To Build a Fire

Books by Melville Cane

January Garden, 1926
Behind Dark Spaces, 1930
Poems: New and Selected, 1938
A Wider Arc, 1947
Making a Poem, 1953
And Pastures New, 1956
Bullet Hunting and Other New Poems, 1960
To Build a Fire, 1964

Co-Editor
The Man from Main Street, 1953
The Golden Year, 1960

To Build a Fire

Recent Poems and a Prose Piece
Melville Cane

Harcourt, Brace & World, Inc. / New York

In memory of:
George Edward Woodberry, 1855-1930
Poet, Teacher, Friend

Many of these poems first appeared in the following publications: *The American Scholar, McCall's, The New York Times, Pages from Tarusa, Poetry in Crystal, Saturday Review, Southwest Review, Sporting News,* and the *University Review.* The prose piece, "A Way of Life," was originally published in *The American Scholar.*

Contents

I

To Build a Fire

The hearth waits,
Clean and bare and ready.

First:
To lay the paper,
A bed of prose to start with.

Then:
Artfully, bit by bit,
Add shavings,
Curling phrases,
Kindling symbols.

Contrive a rhythmic nest of sticks
And crown it with symmetric logs.

Finally:
Loosen and unclog,
That air may flow
And flame may catch.

At This Unlikely Hour

Embers crumble
Mauve to ashen,
Dust of passion
Snows the hearth.

Now the hearth's a grave,
Save for an unsuspected spark
That lurks and circumvents the dark,
And bursts to flower
At this unlikely hour.

By One, Unsure

My feet toe in, as Indians' do,
A natural gait,
And as I track across the snow,
Pursuing fate,
My thoughts turn inward, shutting out
The world's distractions roundabout.

I pause a step and gaze behind
To note a pattern well defined,
Stampings from a special mint
As personal as fingerprint.

The course between, a winding path
Of strait and unassuming breadth,
By one, unsure of destinies,
Who swerves within parentheses.

No Need of Shade

October.
Feebler,
The sun has banked its fires;
A season lost,
Expires.

No longer need
Of shade:
Now, to denude.

Invoke the midnight frost
Forthwith to shrivel and nip
And thoroughly, finally strip
Each branch, each bough.

Now elm and birch declare
Their prime anatomy,
Their essence, wintry-bare,
For all to see.

Mowing the Lawn

With gentle purr
And even whir
Blade
Meets blade
In a bright cascade.

Robins flutter down the path,
Peck and play
In the fresh delectable aftermath
Of soft green spray
This sweet June day.

Lincoln

We have seen the face too often;
We have grown mechanical
And no longer see.

We have taken the image for granted,
A four-cent postage stamp;
We are blinded by habit,
Calloused by usage.

Pause reverently,
Citizen of the Republic,
Stand at a fitting distance,
Recover the image,
Rediscover this man.

An Idea Escapes

Soundless,
A rare and golden butterfly
Swam on air about my head,
Wafted,
Drifted,
And settled on a petal.

Breathless,
All-set,
I raised,
I poised
The subtile net
And cast
And missed.

Waters of Sound

Sound of bells
On throats of ambling cows
Moves like a lazy brook
Across the meadow
Of a summer afternoon.

Sound of bells,
Clanging, counterclanging, over Chartres,
Mounts to a torrent,
Bursts, and overflows
Its bronze and copper banks.

Cows kneel;
Brook dries;
Last peal;
Torrent dies.

Bees, After Rain

Dormant, their house sodden with rain,
Stunned by sudden sun,
The bees stir, revive,
Charge wildly out of the hive,
Race
Furiously,
Then gloriously
Interlace
A golden skein.

White, Out of Heaven

White, out of heaven
Earthward they veer,
Strewn and driven,
They feather the air;
Whirl in the weather,
Hover and cover,
Hold and enfold
A world now lulled,
Deep under the mould.

E. E. Cummings

Although he chose to sing in lower-case,
A whim, perhaps,
Posterity will reset the type, and place
His name in CAPS.

Robert Frost Ad Libs

Out of Yankee rumination
Wisdom, wit, illumination.

Space and Span

Existence:
Distance,
Germinal
To terminal.

Incomputable,
Inscrutable.
Space and span
For the journey of man.

On Hearing Poets from Many Lands

You spoke your verses, each in alien tongue.
Your syllables
Fell on our ears but failed us, language-poor.

We fumbled at a dim and secret door
That held us separate, like an estranging wall.

It slowly yielded; we could hear a call
From heart to kindred heart, a fervent voice
That rose above all barriers of speech;
And we, at last, could hear
A universal music deep and clear.

Brothers in art, all hail! Let us rejoice
In common song
Until the song shall reach
And sweep these darkened skies, from each to each.

To a Grandson

Out of doors
Wild winter.
Here, within,
Relaxed before the hearth,
We fraternize and commune.

An open span of sixty years,
Two generations long,
We close and bridge.

Blood kin,
But, happier, kindred spirit!
I join you from a calmer century;
You greet me from the future.

Lay fresh coals on
To stay the embers.

II

A Thurber Carnival

The face
Deadpan,
The voice
Deadsober,
The treatment,
The texture,
A tricky mixture
Of overtones and understatement.

You're at the entry
Of a bewildering country.
Here,
There's much of import to impart
And more than meets the callous ear.

Observe the horse *behind* the cart,
Absorb the shocks
Of paradox.

Discover the uncommon sense
That lurks around irrelevance,
And witness man's fatuity
When shackled to congruity;

And chuckle at the irony
That salts the human comedy,
And revel in that airy land,
That daffy, quite-contrary land,
Where Thurber's sly executors
Unreel their mad non sequiturs.

At the Movies

Expertly
They've fused their skills,
Writers, actors,
Designers, directors;
Done what they've set out to do,
Contrived
A product, achieved
A show to entertain us.

The house darkens,
We settle in our seats,
Take in
A scene upon a screen.

The play was over long before we entered.

The excitement of a curtain slowly rising,
The electric shock of drama in the making,
We'll never share.
The boards will stay forever bare
And barren.

There'll be no stir
Of an opening night,
And no applause for the star,
And no "oh, oh"! when the heroine
Vainly gropes for a cue,
Or the tense, emotional ingénue
Fluffs her lines,
And the phone won't ring
And the lamp won't light.

Here, within its celluloid confines,
We gaze upon
A scene upon a screen.

Chancy Weather

The sparkle of this April afternoon
Has dwindled dull and sullen.
It looks like rain,—
Indeed it may rain soon,—
Those clouds are surely ominously swollen,
And yet,
A breeze may rise and puff them off again.

For here goes April with her chancy weather,
The skies obedient to her least caprice,
Whether she calls for sun or shower or whether
She teases them, uncertain of her choice.

The damsels scuttle down the avenue
A-click on spiky heels; they heed the threat,
They act before the fact, as damsels do,
Unfurl umbrellas to outwit the wet.

The non-existent wet. The menace thins,
Recedes, a hint of shine pokes through.
Umbrellas furled again as brightness wins,
The girls click on, along the avenue.

Violets, Asparagus

Violets have sneaked into the asparagus bed
And mockingly taken over.

Who says they're modest and shy?

I find them shockingly brazen, ill-bred,
Rapacious,
Pernicious,
Ruinous, hateful and sly.

I can cope fairly well with clover
And the average run of weeds,
But gracious!
How the infernal genus breeds!

There's a time and a place for beauty,
But why this bed? Oh why
Must it make this spot its very own
Instead of a suitable mossy stone,
Half-hidden from the eye?

Conversation Piece

"And what, may I ask, do *you* do?"

Not having gathered my name
(It wouldn't have lent any meaning),
She reached for an opening move.

"I'm a poet," I said, without stressing,
As merely an item of fact.

She countered on me with a challenge:
"Isn't that a debatable matter
And something for others to judge?"

"I'm afraid you've read into my answer
Far more than the answer purports.
I simply asserted my calling;
Of my worth you've seen fit to presume.

"Had I given my name as a painter
You'd have taken it matter-of-course,
Without any tone of defiance
And without any question of art.

"You asked, and I answered your question
As any a workman might.
The better or worse of the product?
That's not on the cards tonight."

Buttonwoods in November

Manhattan is hospitable to buttonwoods,
It welcomes them, says "come and settle here."
They act with favor on the invitation,
Hole in, along the side streets of the town,
Endure the nuisances of urban living,
And, somehow, thrive and flourish.

Buttonwoods are grateful, neighborly folks;
A strong devotion to the public weal
Impels them to an annual contribution:
All summer long and well into the fall
They service hot pedestrians with shade.

Right now they're messing streets with autumn litter,
But no one dreams of handing out a ticket.

Spring Raindrops

Spring raindrops
Prick dull puddles
With sharp, pointillistic
Needles.

Within the sprightly spatter
A pattern looms;
Nature, it seems,
Has gone artistic—
A la
Seurat.

Hurrah
For Seurat!

De Mortuis Nil Nisi Bonum

According to his obit, he
Was noted for his probity,
But I, who held a closer view,
Could tell the world a thing or two.

At the Ball Park

1. Night Game

Lights are on.
Night spreads blue on the park,
Covers bleachers, clears the dark
Of the diamond. Out for fun,
The coatless crowd sweats
Happily. "Cigars, cigarettes!"
Hotdogs, Cokes.
"Get your official score cards, folks!"

Silence!
"Our National Anthem," canned.

At their places
In the outfield, at the bases,
Players stand
Statuelike, caps in hand;
Four umps,
Stiff as pumps.

The engine brays the final bars
Against the moon, the August stars.
The fans uncork their automatic roars.

"Play ball!"

2. Breakdown

"Our National Anthem!"

The fans wriggle out of their seats,
Reluctantly patriotic.
Players, umpires
Pose at attention.

The machine grinds,
Splutters a few sour notes,
Wheezes, goes dead.

The fans fidget, waiting.

Over the loud-speaker
A voice ominous, solemn:
"We regret
That, due to mechanical trouble,
We are unable to . . ."

The fans, relieved,
Sink into their seats
With the first pitch.

Facts

The ginkgo's a tree,
The bronco's a beast,
Facts which, to me,
Don't matter the least.

The junco's a bird,
The Banquo's a ghost,
Facts—take my word—
I can bear with, at most.

The bunco's a cheat,
Flamenco's a dance,
Facts one should meet
With a cool nonchalance.

The Ea-gull

The Ea-gull
(Bald,
So-called)
Bulks far bigger
Than the Sea-gull.
He cuts a figger
Monumental, rea-gull.

It would be less than lea-gull
To invea-gull
An unassuming sea-gull
For a contest with an ea-gull.
He isn't in the same league with an ea-gull.

And neither is a bea-gull.

The Significance of "What"

Hospitality is of two kinds,
Cautious and generous.

Take two cases.

The cautious host
Salutes his guest
With
"*Would* you like something to drink?"

Does he harbor
The secret hope
Of a refusal?

The generous host
Commits himself in advance,
Narrows the issue
To
"*What* will you have to drink?"

A stupendous distinction,
That contingent "would"
Against
That unequivocal "what."

London in August

London,
Dun, dun,
Sky's dun,
Sun's done—
Heigh-ho, the damp and the drear!

Oh, to be so *un*done,
Never to be sunned on!
Shun November, London,
Now that August's here.

New Yorkers

Boobs
Who mole in tubes
And mate in cubes.

Note for Book Publishers

A proper blurb
Should wear the curb
Of purest truth, and verbally
Be free of all hyperbole.

Cerebral Poet

He plans so well, so tightly in advance
The poem he means to do,
No intuition stands the slightest chance
Of wriggling through.

Spots and Stripes

The leopard, uncomplaining of his lot,
Is disinclined to change a single spot—
Quite sensibly, the leopard wouldn't,
Because he knows he couldn't.

The zebra, though condemned to prison-stripes,
Is philosophical and never gripes.

But man, rebellious and tormented biped,
Grapples with fate, unspotted and unstripéd.

H. & B.

Huntley
Utters
The news
More bluntly
Than Brinkley.

Brinkley
Twitters
And coos
More twinkly.

Lady in the Park

(Suggested by a New Yorker *drawing)*

The dear old lady,
Victorian, violet-veined,
Violet-clad and parasoled,
Advances on her usual path to a shady
Bench in the park, disposes
Her neat self with nice propriety,
Now ready to dispense
Today's beneficence.

Beggarly and greedy,
Querulous squirrels
Fidget and frisk expectantly.

The gracious lady smiles indulgently,
Unclasps her broidered reticule
And from its amplitude
Extracts a store of obdurate food
And a tool
To attack it with.

Sweet innocence, for whom the news is lacking
That squirrel-teeth are well-equipped for cracking.

She bursts the shells, loosens the tasty meat;
They snap it up, a-skitter at her feet.
Nut-drunk, their little bellies full,
They breathe ingratitude and ridicule.

The lady shuts an empty reticule,
Raises her pretty parasol,
Rises and goes away
For another day.

III

Within the Dark

I search to find you in the shining day.
In vain.
This shallow radiance
Advances merely to the outer eye,
Reveals no deeper than the natural scene
Of earth to sky
And then lets down its screen.

Beneath, behind,
My vision fails
(Your vision veiled)
And I'm undone and blind.

Now darkness spreads and swells the dark within.
I close the door and move across the room
You brightened once, now tenanted by gloom.
Oh, dare I hope that what has been
May come to pass again!

I draw the curtains, strike a flickering match,
Linger before the fireplace,
Wait for the wood to catch,
Invoke the gradual flame, the missing face.

I seek a light that lies beyond the sun,
(Nor here, within this fire) a sacred source
That emanates from blackness and that runs
Along no earthbound course.

The embers sag, the rose dissolves to ash,
The hovering darkness deepens and surrounds,
And I am stayed and heartened by the hush,
The gathering calm, the quietude profound.

Beneath this calm a hidden current stirs;
A faint, insistent rumor on the night,
Whispers of memory, a messenger's
Annunciation heralded in light.

The rumor grows; I reconstruct the scene:
Your final presence here, the season, late
October, golden-leaved; our world serene.
We sat, as I do now, before the grate,

The room unlit, as now, the fading glow
Defining, as it spread, your shadowy form.
Your hand reached mine; we were contented so;
And we were close and intimate and warm.

And we were stilled and captive in the peace
That welled from silence and that held us free
To fathom love, to salvage and release
The rich deposit of our constancy.

This was our harvest time, our ripened years,
A fruitage formed and firmed of mutable skies
Now warmed with joy, now watered deep with tears.
(Too swift, alas, the frost!) Our autumn dies.

We stirred and eased our clasp; I slowly rose,
Flicked on the light and sparked your cigarette.
You smiled: "Let's have some music; yours to choose."
I set the record of a Brahms quartet,

While you stood up to fetch your sewing box,
Then settled down domestically to heal
The laundry's wounds. The task of mending socks
For you was neither boredom nor ordeal.

Whether to build a fire, broil a steak,
Arrange a bowl of peonies, restore
A frazzled cushion or a cracked antique,
You were at home with each familiar chore.
I poked the embers, fed the struggling flare,
Our talk ran on—promise of years to come,
My poems to be, your classes on the Square,
Or gaily sailing to Byzantium.

We were there, completely together, close and sure,
Single in feeling, one in flavor and grain,
Rapt in an exquisite, rarefied aura of pure
Lumination. Never to bless us again.

Midnight stole in and caught us by surprise.
We roused ourselves to take a look at the weather;
We stepped into the deep outdoors; the skies
Loomed clean and crisp, the stars sang together.

Aglow, we sauntered back. I locked the door,
Snapped on the upstairs light. "Good night!" . . . "Sleep
    well!"
Your farewell country slumber. Nevermore
The country joys, the home you loved so well.

An Antique Dealer Drops By

The car slowed down,
Eased off the highway,
Turned into the driveway,
Threaded hidden behind the trees,
Curved, and gently halted
In the open, toward the house.

It didn't look like any friend's or neighbor's.
It was a black car,
A bulgy limousine,
The front seat for people,
The back for carting,
As ample as a hearse.

I wondered as the man stepped out,
Whether he'd lost his way and needed direction,
Or what new gadget he hoped to trap me with.

"Good afternoon, sir:
May I introduce myself?"
I knew 'twas business before I'd read his card.

Walter Brackett,
Authentic Antiques,
Bristol, Connecticut.

"Authentic antiques,"
I pondered, over the card,
"That fits me to a T,
Provided, of course, four score and three
Will qualify."
The humor, if you'd call it that, escaped him.

To cut him off before he'd start his spiel,
I plumped out:
"You're wasting time on me. I'm not a prospect.
Whatever's here will have to do for a spell."

"I haven't come to sell; the car is empty,"
He countered with, "and waiting to be loaded.
You've got me wrong, I'm figuring to buy.

"I'd pay good money for a piece or so
I might be interested in. You see,
I know your things, I'm not a stranger here.
Three summers back, it's surely that by now,
I dropped around. Your missus came to the door,
Was kind to show me in. I well remember
The curly-maple beds, the piecrust table,
The walnut highboy and the wing chair
She picked up at a bargain, so she said,
While on a scouting jaunt up Ipswich way.
Right proud she was of all those lucky finds,
And with good reason, too; she sure had taste."

He hesitated, ventured on, and added:
"It must be lonesome now, with her away."

Shyly he paused, uncertain.
Commercialism had faded from his voice.
His sympathy was genuine, I felt,
Like that of an old friend.

I welcomed him, not in the hope of any
Spiritual food he might provide,
But rather as a sounding board. I'd kept
Within myself too long; I stood in need
Of simple conversation back and forth,
A chance to breathe more freely.

It's easier to loose one's tongue with a stranger
Passing by, not apt to meet again,
Than someone you feel close to. So I found
Myself replying:

"Lonesome, of course, at times, but not alone.
There's quite a difference there.
She's still about in every part of the place,

In every room of the house, and down below
In the garden, too; working on hands and knees
She set the plants to blossom with the seasons.
Each spring they're up again in all their colors—
Her legacy of beauty you might call it.

"Lover of beauty, that might best describe her,
In life as well as art. You should have seen
The state this place was in, a run-down wreck,
When we first came. It posed the sort of problem
That always challenged her imagination:
How to transform chaos into order.
That, I suppose, is what an artist's meant for;
In fact, that's what he lives for.

"And what she lived for, too.
                            Even if you missed
Her paintings on the walls, didn't you feel?—
You couldn't help but feel—you're not just business,
The artist in the color harmonies,
The gift that knew each object's proper setting,
The spirit that created this, a home?"

He turned to answer:
"I've not the words to tell it as you put it,
But still remember how I carried away
The picture this was what a home should be like.
I've found but few to match it."

And I went on:
"You've got me talking more than I had a mind to.
You stopped by here to trade and not to learn
What personally goes on in a man's heart.
Too bad you're out of luck for, when you leave,
You'll leave no better off than when you came.

"Yes,
I'm out of the market now and once for all.
What's here will stay so long as I'll be staying.
To sell off what she dearly brought together
Would be to strip a work of art, to scrap
A labor of love."

He rose and gripped my hand, then walked to the car.

"Come back," I called, "but don't be in a hurry."
He smiled and waved good-bye.

IV

Translations of Russian Poems
by Evgeny Vinokurov

Old Sins

Old sins return to plague us,
To exact their pound of payment.
Is this just?

We were young, rebellious, tough,
But, remember, we were young,
And youth runs headlong,
Heedless of consequences.

Now I'm ready to pay,
But only for what I owe today,
Not for the folly
Of the lad I was.

Hotels

I fear hotels.
The very thought of filling lungs
With poison from unbeaten rugs,
The stale bedroom reek,
Disgusts me.

I fear hotels,
The cruel cold from windows.
Curtains, a lamp, a sofa—
Fake hospitable warmth,
Make a wretched shelter.

But most, I fear hotels
For that unpredictable hour
When, all alone,
Entrapped within four walls,
I'll face the fact
There'll be no checking out.

Fools

The world is full of fools;
In fact,
You'll find choice specimens
Right here in this neighborhood.

Crazy nuts! Dreamers!
Never a haircut,
Eyeglasses spliced with string.

Always dreaming!
Bedcovers pulled up over their ears,
Scared of a noise in a pipe.

Poor fools!
And yet, I wonder
How much I may have missed,
Never having risked
Their eccentricity.

The Woman

The woman, in truth, was bony.
Her shoulders jutted like two right angles,
She was that bony.
Her dress hung limp like a net,
Her earrings fish-weights,
Her hair seemed glued to her scalp.
Shrewd as a lioness,
She cunningly perched her head
On the shelf of her collarbone.
Mysteriously she smiled
A smile that might have scared you,
Save for her redeeming glory,
Warm green eyes,
Wise with compassion,
Fruit of a lived-out life.

Bathing the Children

Thursday's bath day at our place.
How the children love to race
Around the rooms, naked and free!
My wife presides over the weekly dunking;
Skirt securely tucked up,
Arms bare to the elbows,
She's set, and gets to work.

They squeal over her scrubbing,
Squirm under the steam,
(Hair over their eyes),
Squeeze their eyes to keep the soap out,
Shrink, as a basin of water
Plops and shocks and overflows the tub.

My wife drops to her knees and mops the floor.
"No stalling! Wash behind the ears! Out you go!"

They're back in bed, now, naked,
Sheets pulled up over their heads,
Snug.

This Poetry Business

Would you care to know
How it feels and what it means
Being a poetry editor?

Then listen, and I'll spill the beans.
I'm an authority.
I've had it good and plenty.

These birds move in
With a sly, feminine
Gambit; they court you,
They actually woo you,
But when that fails
They assail you.

Each day, from one to five,
This poor slob,
Meaning me,
Stuck to the job,
Multiplying enemies,
Just hoping he'd survive.

All my paltry salary went
Toward the reinstatement
Of friends whom I'd offended.
They'd pass me on the street
And turn their heads
And cut me dead.

I made an odd discovery at last:
That what they wanted most,
Yes, even more than publication,
Was praise,
And then, more praise!
What egos!

And so,
Whenever I turned a manuscript down,
I gave a sedative,
A pill of flattery,
To ease the pain.

They gloried in rejection,
Not dejection.
They'd leave with faces shining
And tears of gratitude.
That was the general attitude.

Even acceptance of a poem was never final.
I'd pass it on to an editorial board.
Their comments fell
Like a burst of artillery shells
On a practice target,
But, by and large, it
Would be voted in.

What characters!
A youth. Writes staircase verse
Like a sectional bookcase.

An old has-been
Sat across from me,
Gasping, a signet ring
On his beefy hand.

A construction worker,
Tall as a bean pole,
Overalls caked with paint and lime,
Put down his cap—
It stuck to the desk.
Leaving, he had to yank it free.

Then the story
Of the corpulent lady:

"My children have the whooping cough,
My husband has no sensitivity.
I write in bursts!
How else, when there's cooking
To do and shopping,
And no help?
Alone, alone."

And that oddball;
With a wild gleam
In his piercing eyes,
He crazily demanded:
"Appoint me Poet Laureate
Of the Soviet Union!"

They kept crowding in.
They all wrote poems,
The whole cockeyed world writes poems.
I've grown more and more suspicious.
The odd look of that embassy guard!
And when the high executive
Locks himself in his office
Announcing that he's not to be disturbed?
Is he composing an ode?

Authors come and authors go.
Tons of verse forever flow.
In the sultry, humid weather
Words and phrases melt together—
Sticky fruit-drops in a bag,
All of Russia's on a jag!

I was poisoned from them
And, like a supersaturated solution,
Crystallization began to set in.
And then
The muse emerged in strange seductive guises
Of rhomboids
And octahedrons of assorted sizes.

I might have hated poetry all my life
But for that happy unexpected time
I came across one line. . . .

V

A Way of Life

An invitation to describe one's way of life, had it arrived in the mail, might have hung in the balance; reflection might have counseled rejection as the better part of wisdom. But we are rarely given the gift of reflection in the age of the telephone, and an editor's beguiling voice over the wire presents quite a different matter; one's guard is down and one's ego takes over. So in practically the same sentence, I stated that I had never organized my beliefs or formulated a supporting course of conduct; that, therefore, I felt quite disqualified for the task; and that—not therefore, but nevertheless—I'd be glad to make a try at it.

My decision has relevance since it represents a changing attitude toward new adventures. Ten years or so ago, either from inertia or some other negating demon, I should certainly have shied away promptly. Now, as time grows shorter and one's machinery tends to become rusty and slow down, one is challenged with the prospect of progressive deterioration and decline.

How to meet this challenge is the problem which confronts each of us regardless of his years, but more urgently the aging. What resources, spiritual, intellectual, emotional, can we summon in order to invest the tenuous future with vitality, value and felicity? In short, how can we make of life a continuous surge of renewal and fruition? To this momentous question each of us will give his answers according to his lights.

That I might indeed own a philosophy of life, in the august connotations of the phrase, had never occurred to me until recently. Even now I doubt that what goes for a philosophy is much more than a serviceable formula for survival. I have never deliberately reduced my thoughts to a system or creed; that seems too self-conscious a performance and too presumptuous. My training as a lawyer in logical exposition has never extended to methodical speculation concerning the universe or my role in it. That's not saying that I don't speculate; I have, and I do.

Intimations from the outside have now prodded me toward self-examination. Critics have noted a "philosophical" strain in my poems—they've used that awesome word—and a review of my latest volume in the New York *Times* appeared under the startling head "A Lyric Philosopher."

Here I need point out that consciously I rarely write so-called philosophical poetry. My poems for the most part derive not so much from a set theme or subject as from intuitions, sensations, feelings momentarily captured. These I develop to no other end than that the product shall be as perfect aesthetically as an imperfect artist can make them. If the product should give off a philosophic overtone, it derives from the artifact and not from any initial intent. The overtone is a by-product.

Now, re-examining my work, I must admit that the critics may have a point. Without having been aware of it before, I now discover many cherished convictions in my verse.

A way of life, to adopt a less heavy phrase, is not something one receives ready-made to be copied, or something one frames and hangs on the office wall, like Kipling's "If." A way of life is a force whose origin goes back to infancy and whose growth stops only at the grave. Its contour and content issue, among other things, from background, temperament, and the variety and unpredictability of our experiences. Our unique personal characteristics, whether inherited or early acquired, form doubtless a major initial influence.

In my own case, my guess would be that I am probably cheerful by nature, and that no matter how clouded the horizon for the time being, cheerfulness remains the prevailing color of my outlook. It follows that cheerfulness by its very warmth breeds optimism; it likewise carries within itself the strain of humor, and humor in its deepest sense and significance is but another name for perspective. To see life both steadily and whole, in Arnold's phrase, is both the beginning and the end of wisdom.

Cheerfulness, to repeat, breeds optimism, and optimism is born of faith. Faith for me is the unreasoned conviction that however incomprehensible the source of creation may be, meaning lies at the heart of the mystery. And whatever may be the secret of divinity, I hold that the universe was conceived and fashioned not haphazardly, but with plan, system, and purpose, and that we, here on earth, have been appointed to be the instruments and agents of the plan.

So circumstanced, each one of us is charged with a heavy responsibility. I maintain that within every human soul there resides the essence and the presence of divinity, and that our main if not sole excuse for being rests on our assuming the obligation to be faithful to our destiny.

I further believe that each of us is endowed at birth not only with the capacity for good but also with the counterforce of evil. Evil I define loosely and not in doctrinal or theological terms as anything tending to seduce us from our ordained course or to impair or destroy our will and our search toward self-realization.

Evil assumes Protean dissemblances and disguises, too many indeed for enumeration. I shall set down a few examples out of my own experience, though not necessarily in the order of their importance. Some have crept into my poems.

Evil, however, need not be evil inexorably. With one emotionally caught in its coils it loses its hold when the victim confronts it objectively. Objectivity frees one from frustrating involvement and thereby restores to the person his saving detachment.

One habitual pattern of evil, to illustrate, appears in the masochistic aspect of "the backward glance," by which is meant self-flagellation over past failures, whether of lost opportunities or of nonsuccess in performance. Here again cool detachment is needed to free the psyche from a sterile and harmful condition. I stress the danger in these few lines:

> Beware the vain lament,
> The hunger for what's spent.
> This is dead-sea fruit
> And ashes to the taste.
> Quash it with your foot.
> What is past is past.

Evil thrives on loss of self-control, whether in anger, grief or other emotional disturbance. Evil delights in blind suffering. Suffering is without value unless one is able to ask in the aftermath of reflection: "Why have I suffered?" Then and not till then can one profit from the experience. To approach the problem in quite another way, paradoxically, one can overpower suffering through surrendering to it. I've attempted to express this in the following short poem:

GIVE WAY TO GRIEF

Give way to grief,
And, unashamed,
Abandon stoic fortitude a while.
Set free, a while, the soul,
Better to bear its load.

Tears unshed are stones upon the heart
That choke the healing stream.

Unlock the flood-gates;
Loose the waters.
Give way, and cope with grief.

And evil in perhaps its most seductive guise assails us where we may be especially vulnerable, in our relation to the world outside and to our fellow men. A poem, "The Plausible," begins with these lines:

The devil
With malign
Design
Is out to scale mankind to a common level.

Conformity, clearly, is the relentless archenemy of the individual. How to outwit its stratagems and elude its toils will call for the most untiring vigilance, the keenest awareness. For

Beneath the alluring guise of reason
(Man's weakness for the plausible
The comfortable solution)
It spreads its poison.

But even more strongly than on reason does conformity press its specious appeal on conscience. Our business is to be alert against any false reading of our obligations, in the name of duty, to collective expedience; against any surrender of personality, our qualitative singularity, to quantitative commonality.

For our mores are grounded in the general need for cooperative security. To what extent are they based on principle, to what extent merely convenient and changeable rules for communal living? And to what extent should we, need we, subscribe and give assent? How far shall duty govern, how far self-interest and self-preservation? We must recognize, for our own protection, that the mores derive from compromise, from mutual accommodation to general needs, that they represent adjustment to an undefined impersonal average. Devoid of absolute standards of character and behavior, they fail to apprehend the highest reach or to take into account man's ideal quest for perfectibility.

Man's concern, therefore, is to defend his identity, to preserve his own unique image. He must resist the pressure of convention which demands that he put on a collective mask. As citizens in a democracy, alike prizing its blessings and gratefully sharing its burdens, we must never forget its essential meaning. Democracy is not a mere abstraction but an instrument for liberating and insuring the spiritual endowment, indeed, the birthright, of every individual.

Freedom to doubt, to dissent, to be different and stand separate from the mass, is not only a sacred right but an opportunity and responsibility for advancing the common lot. The strength of a civilization is to be measured by the qualities of those who compose it.

How can one specify his techniques for facing the future? One needs, though one hesitates, to be autobiographical.

Being in my ninth decade, I must, inevitably, expectedly, confront the matter of "old age." I reject the phrase with its suggestion that it represents a limited compartment of time requiring special and desperate treatment. In that phrase I find menace, apprehension, consciousness of the Grim Reaper's shadow over one's shoulder. This symbol of the Reaper, which I attach to the phrase, grimly bent on cutting me down, is far too unsettling for peace of mind and a constructive life. I am likewise annoyed when in answer to a question about his health a contemporary may say, with a touch of depreciation, "Pretty good for an old man," when he really has nothing to complain of.

Our later years, assuming that one has developed a healthy attitude toward life, carry on a natural, unbroken continuity with what has gone before. We should approach them not in crisis but with the serenity that accompanies the passing of the seasons.

Neither am I happy with the equivocal term *retirement;* it is too heavily weighted with a sense of withdrawal. Withdrawal from what? To what? For what? Retirement can mean retreat or surrender. It *should* mean escape from impedimenta to the vantage ground of fulfillment.

I have arrived at a few conclusions on what to avoid and what to welcome, usable tools for progress. Here is the list, platitudes and all:

The need to overcome negative attitudes and negative emotions. For example, a closed mind, any waste or leakage of energy.

Not to anticipate disaster or failure, but to make each day sufficient unto itself. Again, the conservation of psychic energy.

To learn from suffering and thereby to transcend it.

To thrive on the emotional friction created by difficulty and disappointment.

To keep in sound physical condition through proper exercise—walking, golfing, gardening—and through sensible, and therefore enjoyable, choice of food, drink, and tobacco.

To meet one's fellow beings as equals, neither with sufferance nor with condescension.

To establish a rhythm and tempo of detachment, which inherently creates a sense of perspective and the larger view.

To keep open the pores of the mind, and to keep flexible and resilient the antennae of intuition, sensation, and feeling.

Not to fancy that an accumulation of years will qualify one as a Nestor. Regrettably, one may even be a tiresome Polonius. Similarly, to be sure not to cultivate the stoop of self-importance.

To approach each fresh problem with an honest skepticism and the wish to arrive at truth.

To summon fresh energies from untapped sources.

And, most important, constantly to strive for further light in one's search for the true self.

I cap what I have been saying with a quotation from Lord David Cecil's essay on Joseph Conrad which cautions never "to allow oneself to be cowed by the danger and disaster of existence into surrendering that faith in the value of individual nobility which is implanted in the human soul at birth."

Finally, what I most deeply believe may be found in the following poem, which appeared twenty-two years ago, and which probably says as much in its brevity as has been sought gropingly in these pages.

THE TASK

How to cope
With the flight of hope;

Under despair
How to endure
(Endure! Endure!)

And be more than a leaf
On the gale of grief,

And perceive, as only a fraction,
The pain and distraction.

How, in the perilous instant,
To hold, how dimly, the constant;

How dimly,
The way, the meaning, the mystery.

How, in the clutch of extinction,
Still to function, human!

This is the task, the prayer,—that I may save
The suffering god within, that he may live,
And greatly live, beyond the grave.